Transport

Paul Dowswell

Heinemann
LIBRARY

www.heinemann.co.uk/library

Visit our website to find out more information about Heinemann Library books.

To order:

☎ Phone 44 (0) 1865 888066

🖹 Send a fax to 44 (0) 1865 314091

💻 Visit the Heinemann Bookshop at www.heinemann.co.uk/library to browse our catalogue and order online.

First published in Great Britain by Heinemann Library, Halley Court, Jordan Hill, Oxford OX2 8EJ, a division of Reed Educational and Professional Publishing Ltd. Heinemann is a registered trademark of Reed Educational & Professional Publishing Limited.

OXFORD MELBOURNE AUCKLAND JOHANNESBURG BLANTYRE
GABORONE IBADAN PORTSMOUTH NH (USA) CHICAGO

Designed by Tinstar Design (www.tinstar.co.uk)
Illustrations by Nicholas Beresford-Davies & Martin Griffin
Originated by Ambassador Litho Ltd
Printed in Hong Kong/China

ISBN 0 431 13231 3
05 04 03 02 01
10 9 8 7 6 5 4 3 2 1

British Library Cataloguing in Publication Data
Dowswell, Paul
        Transport. – (Great Inventions)
        1. Transportation – History
        1. Title
        388'.09

Acknowledgements
The Publishers would like to thank the following for permission to reproduce photographs:
AKG: p20, 31, 38, Erich Lessing p10; Aviation Images: p42; Aviation Picture Library: Austin J Brown p36; Corbis: pp4, 5, 6, 14, 15, 28, 35, 37, 41; Culture Archive: p27; Empics Ltd: Jon Buckle p25; Hulton Getty: pp9, 10; Mary Evans Picture Library: pp13, 23, 26; Motoring Picture Library: p29; R. N. Submarine Museum: p16; Science and Society: pp12, 18, 19, 22, 24; Science Photo Library: US Library of Congress p33, David Parker p40, Jim Amos p43

Cover photographs: Empics (l), Photodisc (tr), Corbis (br)

Every effort has been made to contact copyright holders of any material reproduced in this book. Any omissions will be rectified in subsequent printings if notice is given to the Publisher.

Any words appearing in the text in bold, **like this**, are explained in the Glossary.

Contents

Introduction

Getting from one place to another is an essential human activity. Without our ability to travel, human settlements would be cut off from each other. Some isolated parts of the world, such as Australia, New Zealand and the Pacific islands, are populated by humans only because their distant ancestors used primitive boats to get there more than 50,000 years ago.

Primitive transportation

The first travellers used their feet to go anywhere. The dirt tracks and primitive bridges that marked popular routes are transport's first inventions. Boats were developed long before land transport, giving seaside and river communities a great advantage over other communities. From the earliest times water was seen as the best way to transport heavy goods. This is still the case today. The biggest mobile objects ever made are enormous supertankers and **cargo** ships.

Animals were **domesticated** around 9000BC, and donkeys, camels, oxen and horses were used to carry goods and people. The invention of the wheel in 3500BC, and the animal-drawn wagons and chariots that followed, was the most significant development in transport for the next 5000 years.

These camels are being used to carry people and goods across the Sahara Desert. Humans have been using animals as a form of transportation for at least 9000 years.

Steam power

The first practical steam engine was invented in 1712, and its impact on transport in the late 18th and early 19th centuries was phenomenal. At sea, steam power freed the sailor from his 5000-year dependence on the wind and the tides. On land, **steam-powered** locomotives rapidly transformed the civilizations that used them, offering long-distance transport that was quick, cheap and reliable. Britain had the first passenger railway in the world in 1825. By 1850 a staggering 100 million passenger journeys were being made in Britain every year.

The engine as we know it

Another revolution even more significant arrived in 1885. Karl Benz produced the first petrol-driven **internal combustion engine**, which he fitted to a modified horse carriage. Today, barely a hundred years later, there are estimated to be 500 million cars in use. The internal combustion engine also allowed for the invention of other forms of transport including the aeroplane and helicopter. The jet engine, invented in 1930, completed a half-century of extraordinary developments in transport technology. Today, passenger jets can travel from London to New York in an unbelievable three hours, and **military** jets can fly a mile in less than three seconds.

Many inventions arrived independently of one another in different countries. Others, such as the steam locomotive, are a product of many different ideas combined, to make for a distinct new form of transport technology.

Concorde can carry passengers from London to New York in three hours. The first powered flight was made by the Wright Brothers in 1903. Less than 60 years later, aircraft could fly at twice the speed of sound.

Bridges, 10,000BC

The first bridges would have been logs laid across narrow streams. However, when people began to **domesticate** animals, something wider was needed for them to cross. This led to the development of the first constructed bridges.

Pillar and beam

The pillar and beam bridge was made by building pillars at regular intervals, and laying beams across from one pillar to the next. The pillars were made of stone, and the beams from stone slabs or timber. In the 4th century BC, Greek historian Herodotus described a pillar and beam bridge in Babylon (now modern Iraq). It had 100 stone piers, timber beams, and stretched over 200 metres (660ft). Most early pillar and beam bridges had short spans.

Suspension bridge

With the suspension bridge, the entire structure is suspended over a drop, and there are no piers. The first suspension bridges were made from vines and creepers, which were tied to tree trunks on either side of a gorge or river bank. Such bridges were common in Ancient India, China and Africa, where they can still be seen today.

This early pillar and beam bridge in Dartmoor, England, was probably built by the Celts. A new bridge has been built behind it.

Pontoon bridge

Pontoon bridges work in the same way as pillar and beam bridges, only boats are used as pillars. King Xerxes of Persia (now called Iran) and his army were reported to have crossed the Bosphorus in Turkey, in 480BC, using a pontoon bridge made of 300 boats. These bridges rarely lasted for more than a few days.

The Romans

Many of the Romans' bridges were wooden, and have not survived. Others were made of stone, and you can still see some of them today. The Romans perfected a new building technique involving an arch, which made a much stronger and safer bridge. They also used the arch to make aqueduct bridges, which carried water into their towns. The discovery of a water-proof cement called pozzolana, allowed them to make concrete for underwater foundations, and the development of the **coffer dam** became an essential bridge-building technique.

The modern day

Bridge-building changed little from Roman times until the 19th century. Then great changes were made thanks to the availability of iron, steel and reinforced concrete. Woven wire made it possible to build long suspension bridges. Other types of bridges include swing bridges, vertical lift bridges and drawbridges, but the pillar and beam, arch, suspension and coffer dam techniques are still used for most bridges today.

Building an arch
Arches in Roman bridges made them strong and safe. They were built like this:

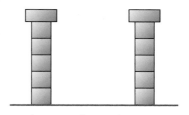

1. A column of stones formed a pier

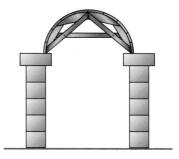

2. An arch-shaped wooden support was built between two columns

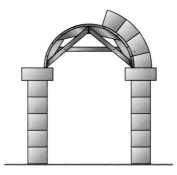

3. Wedge-shaped stones were placed on top of the wooden support

10000BC	c. 400BC	c. 300BC	1841	1998
FIRST LOG BRIDGES IN USE	PILLAR AND BEAM BRIDGES IN USE IN MIDDLE EAST	ROMANS INVENT POZZOLANA, A WATER-PROOF CEMENT	INVENTION OF WOVEN IRON CABLE MAKES POSSIBLE DEVELOPMENT OF MODERN SUSPENSION BRIDGES	WORLD'S LARGEST BRIDGE COMPLETED – AKASHI KAIKYO BRIDGE, JAPAN IS 6750 FEET LONG

Roads, 4000BC

When cities and towns first began to spring up around 4000BC, routes between them slowly emerged in the form of dirt tracks. One of the world's first cities, Ur, in the Middle East, was thought to have paved streets. If this is true, these would have been the world's first proper roads.

Roman roads

The Minoans of Crete built a limestone-paved road around 2000BC, and the Ancient Egyptians and Babylonians also built roads. But the Romans were the greatest road builders of ancient times. Their roads were so hard-wearing some are still in use today, and the **network** of roads the Romans left behind form the basis of Europe's road and rail lines.

In all, the Romans constructed 29 major routes totalling over 80,000km (53,000 miles) of road, all of which were linked to Rome. Once a country had been conquered, road building swiftly followed. These roads enabled armies to march quickly to trouble spots, but they were also used by traders and ordinary travellers.

Building a Roman road
Roman roads were laid down between the shortest, flattest route available. Trees and turf were cleared and a wide trench around 1m (3ft) was dug. This was filled with four layers of stones.

The road was cambered (curved) so rain water would drain away to the sides

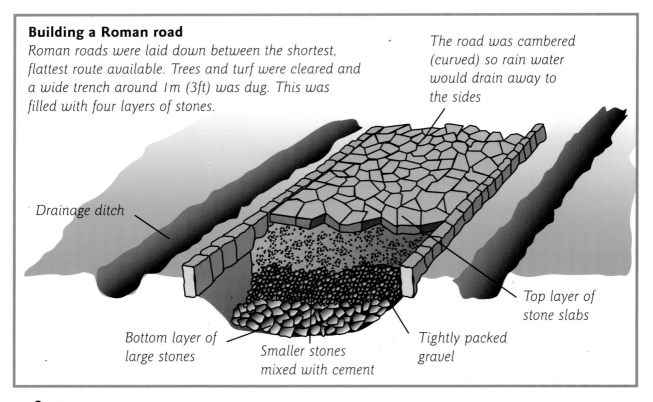

Drainage ditch

Top layer of stone slabs

Bottom layer of large stones

Smaller stones mixed with cement

Tightly packed gravel

Turnpikes

When the Roman Empire collapsed, its roads gradually fell into disrepair. Only in the mid-18th century did governments begin to make improvements in their roads. In Britain, **turnpike** companies maintained stretches of road, but charged travellers to use them. In the United States, turnpike companies also maintained some roads. But when railroads were introduced in the 19th century, so few made a profit they were usually run by local councils.

The road to the motorway

Scottish road builder John Loudon McAdam (1756–1836) developed a method that was adopted throughout Europe. The roads were made of three layers of small stones placed over flattened and well-drained soil that was raised above the surrounding ground. After 1830, railways became an increasingly popular way to travel, and many roads once again fell into disrepair.

1930s German autobahn. The arrival of fast moving motorcars meant that existing roads had to be rapidly improved.

The popularity of the bicycle and the arrival of motor transport at the latter end of the 19th century forced governments to improve roads. A layer of tar or asphalt was placed over the existing surface, and topped with stone chips to improve grip. Governments began to build motorways which had hard-wearing concrete surfaces ideal for heavy use by fast-moving traffic. The first high-speed motorway was built in Berlin between 1913 and 1921. Between the 1930s and 1960s, motorway routes sprang up all over Europe and North America.

4000BC	2000BC	c. 500BC–AD476	1816	1913–1921
PAVED STREETS IN THE CITY OF UR	MINOANS BUILD LIMESTONE ROAD IN CRETE	ROMANS BUILD THE FINEST ROADS IN THE ANCIENT WORLD	JOHN LOUDON McADAM DEVELOPS THREE-LAYER ROAD, WHICH IS ADOPTED THROUGHOUT EUROPE	FIRST HIGH-SPEED MOTORWAY BUILT IN BERLIN

Wheel, c. 3500BC

The wheel arrived in human history around 3500BC. In one of history's most curious twists, the wheel was unknown to such civilizations as the Incas and Aztecs of South America and the North American Indian tribes, until Europeans arrived in the 16th century – a whole 5000 years after it had been invented.

The first wheel?

The first wheel may have been a potter's wheel. Such devices enabled clay containers to be made much quicker. Historical records show potter's wheels and ox-drawn carts arrived at around the same time – 3500BC. Both came from the Middle Eastern civilizations of Mesopotamia and Sumeria.

It is likely that the wheel evolved from the roller. Rollers such as tree trunks had been used to move heavy loads like building stones and boats. Eventually, someone must have thought about putting the roller on another early invention, the sledge. This could be pulled along by animals, such as oxen, using a yoke. This technique was also used to pull ploughs over agricultural land.

Eternal circle

Because the wheel is circular, it can turn continuously. Only one small part of the wheel is in contact with the ground at any one time. But wheels also require a lot of skill to build. A carpenter would have to make a perfect circle, and have to join the circle to the **axle** exactly at its mid-point. Any wheel not made accurately, would cause the cart it was attached to, to bob around uncomfortably.

This magnificent 7th century chariot belongs to the Assyrian King Assurbanipal. The sturdy wheels were strong enough to support a platform carrying four men. The chariot was harnessed to two horses.

The first wheels were made of three pieces of carved wood nailed to two connecting boards. Three pieces of wood were used, because trees in the Middle East were rarely big enough to allow the entire trunk to make a wheel. Later, improvements were made. To make the wheel lighter, wood between the axle and outer rim was hollowed out to make spokes. The rim was also strengthened, first with another wooden strip, and later with a thin copper band.

Trade became much easier as goods and people could be carried long distances. Contact with other tribes and civilizations also brought wealth, materials and fresh ideas.

Essential invention

Other than transport, the wheel has had other vital uses. Water wheels helped **irrigate** some of the first farms, allowing crops to be grown on land that would previously never have sustained them. Water wheels also powered flour mills. Before the invention of the steam engine thousands of years later, they also drove textile-making machinery in the first factories of Britain's 18th-century Industrial Revolution.

3500BC	c. 2000BC	16TH CENTURY	1888
WHEEL INVENTED IN MESOPOTAMIA AND SUMERIA	SPOKES WERE DEVISED TO MAKE WHEELS LIGHTER	WHEEL ARRIVES WITH EUROPEANS IN NORTH AND SOUTH AMERICA	JOHN DUNLOP INVENTS THE **PNEUMATIC TYRE**

John Dunlop's son, in 1888, on the first bicycle to have pneumatic tyres.

Sailing ship, 3100BC

As humans spread throughout the world, they made boats with whatever materials were available to them. In Europe good size trees were plentiful, so boats were made of hollowed-out logs. In Egypt, big trees were rare, so woven reeds from the papyrus plant were used. In the Middle East, boats were made of planks and inflated animal hides. All of these vessels were propelled through the water with simple paddles.

The sail and oar

The first sails were probably fitted to Egyptian boats on the Nile, in around 3100BC. A simple sail could catch the wind and push a boat against the river current. Sails were square or rectangular, and set at a right angle along a tall wooden pole called a mast.

Oars were invented around 1500BC. Unlike paddles, which are simply pushed into the water by the user, oars rest on a **pivot** at the side of the boat, which provided a more powerful push through the water. But oars needed oarsmen, who were expensive. Even if they were slaves they still had to be bought and fed. In general, warships made use of the extra speed oars provided. But trading vessels, keen to keep their profits on a voyage as high as possible, still relied on sails to get them from A to B.

This wooden model from around 1300BC shows the type of boat that would carry people and cargo up and down the Nile in Egypt.

Further developments

Over the centuries boats grew sturdier and larger, and bigger sails were fitted. A deep **keel** under the boat also balanced the weight of a tall mast. By Roman times some sea-going ships had two or three sails, and two masts.

From the 13th century onwards, European vessels adopted the 'lateen' sail which had been seen on Arab trading boats. It was triangular and could be set at an angle on the mast. This shape made it much easier for a ship to sail against the wind. Spanish and Portuguese sailors in the 15th and 16th centuries used lateen sails on their great voyages around the world.

A mid-19th-century Clipper. Such vessels could carry 700 passengers, and sailed until faster and more efficient steamships took over.

By the 19th century, huge vessels with several masts and twelve or more sails would carry hundreds of passengers and thousands of tons of **cargo** around the globe. It would take 100 days to travel between Shanghai and London, but at the time this seemed remarkably swift. During the 19th and early 20th centuries, steam-powered paddles, then propellers, gradually replaced the sail.

50,000BC	5000BC	3100BC	1500BC	13TH CENTURY AD
EVIDENCE OF THE FIRST BOATS – DUGOUT CANOES, POWERED BY PADDLES	REED AND WOODEN SHIPS BUILT IN EGYPT AND MESOPOTAMIA	FIRST SAILS USED ON BOATS ON THE RIVER NILE	OAR INVENTED. IT IS THREE TIMES MORE EFFICIENT THAN THE PADDLE	EUROPEAN SHIPS ADOPT ARABIC LATEEN SAILS, WHICH MAKES THEM EASIER TO SAIL INTO THE WIND

Horse transport, 2000BC

Horses were first harnessed to wheeled vehicles around 2000BC. On a good level path, a horse-drawn, four-wheeled wagon could cover 150km (100 miles) a day. Horse-drawn vehicles revolutionized warfare. A warrior on a chariot had a speed and flexibility that an ordinary foot soldier had not. The chariot too could be used as a weapon, if its wheels were fitted with sharp blades called scythes.

Horses allowed information to be carried across a country or **empire**. A series of horses and riders could carry orders from a king, or news of a battle, 300km (190 miles) a day. This speed of communication would not be improved until the 19th century.

Stirrups, reins and saddle

The first-known stirrups (leather or metal hoops for the feet) were used by the Scythians of Asia Minor (now called Turkey) around 380BC. These helped a rider to stay on the horse's back, using their feet and legs. Stirrups were not used in Europe until after Roman times. In around 300BC, the Celts of Northern Europe were using reins and a bit to control their horses. This took advantage of the fact that a horse runs with its head forward: if the head is pulled up, the horse will stop. The first saddles originated in China in the first century AD.

This four-wheel Sumerian wagon is drawn by two horses. It dates from around 2000BC.

Towards the 21st century

For nearly 2000 years **cavalry** was the most feared and effective weapon a commander could employ, until the 20th century brought barbed wire, machine guns and the invention of the tank. The British canals of the 18th century used horses to pull the coal and factory goods which were vital to the success of the **Industrial Revolution**. In 19th-century America, horse-drawn stagecoaches carried settlers to the new western territories. The first combined-harvesters of the early 19th century used teams of up to 30 horses to pull them through the fields.

The days of horse-drawn transport came to an end with the discovery of **steam-power** and the invention of the **internal combustion engine**. Cars, motorbikes, planes and helicopters revolutionized the transport system. Today, horses are still an essential way of carrying people and goods in many developing countries, but in the West they are mostly used for leisure and sport.

Domesticating animals

Animals were first **domesticated** by humans when farms were set up around 9000BC. Cows and sheep were kept for milk, meat, wool and leather. Oxen were used to pull an early type of plough, and a type of small horse called an ass was used to transport people or goods. It could carry a 60kg (132lb) load. Camels too, were used as transport animals. A big camel could carry up to 500kg (1100lbs).

When the United States expanded its borders in the 19th century, the stagecoach was one of the main methods of travel for migrants heading west to the new territories.

2000BC	380BC	300BC	C. AD 100
HORSES HARNESSED TO WHEELED VEHICLES	SCYTHIANS USE STIRRUPS FOR HORSE RIDING	CELTS USE REIN AND BIT TO CONTROL HORSE	SADDLE USED IN CHINA

Submarine, AD 1620

Submarines became one of the most influential weapons of the 20th century, but their invention and development was slow in coming. Alexander the Great (356–323BC) was said to have used some sort of submarine to defend his fleet from attacking divers, and there are records of diving bells being used as early as 200BC.

The first proper submarine was invented by Dutchman Cornelius van Drebel. He based his invention on the ideas of British mathematician William Bourne, who had dreamed up a leather-clad craft, driven through the water by oars. Van Drebel's invention was tried out on the River Thames in London in 1620 with twelve men rowing eight miles (13km) from Westminster to Greenwich. It floated five metres underwater, and a tube to the surface supplied the crew with fresh air. But little more was heard of the submarine for another 150 years.

Van Drebel's submarine. Its 12-man crew managed to row it down the Thames from Westminster to Greenwich.

The 18th century onwards

War spurred on the submarine's development over the next 200 years. A submarine named *Bushnell's Turtle*, after its inventor David Bushnell, tried to blow up a British warship in New York harbour in 1776, during the American War of Independence. The attempt wasn't successful. *The Turtle* was a strange egg-shaped vessel, and it moved by turning a screw **propeller** by hand.

Submarines making use of air- or water-filled ballast tanks to take them above or below the surface were invented in 1801 by American Robert Fulton. Electric motors were first used in 1886, to power the submarines. By the early 20th century, submarines carried a diesel engine to drive them along the surface, and an electric engine to propel them underwater. The diesel engine was much cheaper for long distance travel.

Diesel and electrical engines were an efficient combination that tied in with another technological breakthrough – accurate, effective **torpedoes**, which were invented in 1866. The first use of **periscopes** around the same time meant that the submarine could see to attack from underwater. During the First World War (1914–1918), German submarines were so effective they almost won the war. One, named *U-35*, sank 324 Allied ships.

The introduction of **nuclear power** to submarines in 1954 meant they did not need air to power the engines, and gave these vessels an almost unlimited underwater range. In 1960 the American submarine *USS Triton* travelled underwater all the way around the world in 12 weeks. This and the fact that submarines are not easily detected make them perfect carriers of nuclear missiles.

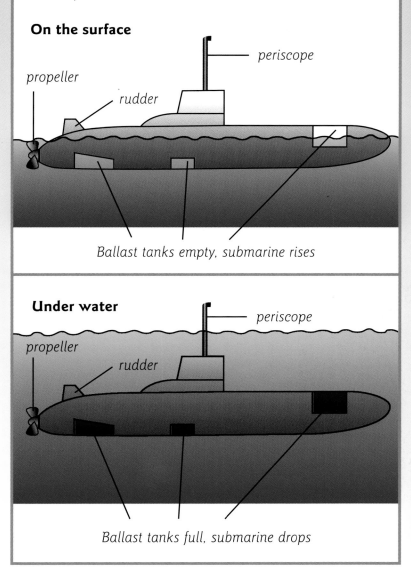

How a submarine works
Submarines rise or drop beneath the sea by flooding or emptying ballast tanks. Introducing water makes the submarine heavier, so it sinks. Expelling the water with compressed air makes the submarine lighter, so it rises to the surface.

On the surface

propeller

periscope

rudder

Ballast tanks empty, submarine rises

Under water

propeller

periscope

rudder

Ballast tanks full, submarine drops

200BC	1620	1776	1886	1914–1918	1954
FIRST RECORDED USE OF DIVING BELLS	CORNELIUS VAN DREBEL'S OAR-POWERED SUBMARINE MAKES ITS FIRST VOYAGE	SUBMARINE FIRST USED IN WARFARE	ELECTRIC MOTOR FIRST FITTED TO SUBMARINE	SUBMARINE ONE OF MOST EFFECTIVE WEAPONS OF FIRST WORLD WAR	NUCLEAR-POWERED SUBMARINE INTRODUCED

Steamship, 1783

For thousands of years, ships had been moved along by oars and sails, and seafarers were reluctant to change from these methods. The first **steam-powered** voyage took place in 1783. Marquis Joffroy d'Abbans took his boat *Peryscaphe* out onto the River Saône in Lyon, France. For 15 minutes, a wheezing, billowing steam engine drove a set of paddles which propelled *Peryscaphe* along. The trip came to an abrupt end when the boat shook to pieces.

In 1790 American inventor John Fitch ran a steamboat on the Delaware River. In 1807 Robert Fulton built the first passenger-carrying steamship, the *Clermont*, which ran between New York and Albany. The *Clermont*, belching smoke and flames, trundled along against the tide and wind, making its 240km (150 mile) journey in 32 hours.

Robert Fulton's Clermont, the first steamship to make regular passenger trips. Its engine powered two paddles either side of the vessel.

Steamships at sea

The first sea-going steamship was built by John and Robert Stevens. In 1809 their boat *Phoenix* took thirteen days to travel between New York and Philadelphia. By 1838, regular Atlantic crossings were being made, although early steamships usually carried both steam engine and sails to make good use of the wind, and in case the engine broke down.

At first, steam engines drove ships with huge paddle wheels, with two on each side, or one at the back. In 1835 the **propeller** took over as the better means of **propulsion**. Paddles were more easily damaged, and lifted out of the water when the sea was rough, but they remained popular with river steamships until well into the 20th century.

Engine improvements during the 19th century demonstrated that steam was better than sail. The first steamboats used wood for fuel, but in 1818 Robert Stevens showed that coal was much more efficient. The **steam turbine** was developed by Charles Parsons in 1884. This forced high-pressure steam over turbine blades, which turned a propeller shaft. This increased the power of the engine and the speed of the ship considerably. By the end of the century, ships were also using two, three and even four propellers, which would prevent a propeller-driven steamship being stranded if its propeller shaft broke.

Today, most ocean-going ships are still powered by steam turbines, and some use **nuclear power** to generate their steam.

British engineer Isambard Kingdom Brunel's The Great Eastern, *at the time, was the largest vessel ever built. Like many early ocean-going steamships it also carried a full set of sails.*

1783	1790	1807	1819	1838	1884
MARQUIS JOFFROY D'ABBANS MAKES FIRST STEAM-POWERED VOYAGE IN *PERYSCAPHE*	JOHN FITCH SAILS A SMALL STEAMBOAT ON THE RIVER DELAWARE	ROBERT FULTON INTRODUCES FIRST STEAMSHIP PASSENGER SERVICE BETWEEN NEW YORK AND ALBANY	*SAVANNAH* IS FIRST STEAMSHIP TO CROSS ATLANTIC, ALTHOUGH IT USES ITS SAILS FOR MUCH OF THE JOURNEY	REGULAR STEAMSHIP SERVICE ACROSS ATLANTIC	CHARLES PARSONS INVENTS THE STEAM TURBINE

Balloon, 1783

The first attempts at flying were usually heroic leaps from tall buildings or cliffs, with aspiring birdmen wearing makeshift feather or wooden wings. These experiments were usually fatal. But the Chinese were able to fly humans on the front of giant kites as early as the 6th century AD. They could be said to have invented the first hang-gliders.

Experiments

In 1709 Father Bartolomeu de Gusmão demonstrated in the royal courtroom of the King of Portugal, João V, how a small balloon could rise up to the ceiling. His invention was based on the fact that hot air rises. The balloon carried a small candle which heated the air inside it, causing it to rise. But, fearing his curtains would be set alight, João ordered a guard to shoot the balloon down.

The first manned balloon flight in November 1783, in a balloon built by the Montgolfier brothers.

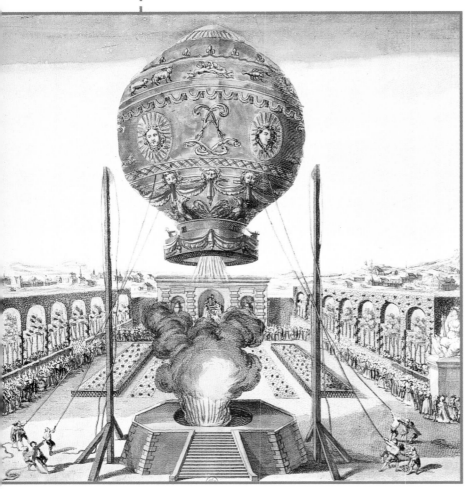

Later that century, two wealthy French brothers, Joseph and Étienne Montgolfier, watched flakes of ash rise above a blazing fire, and noted that up-ended paper bags floated even higher. So in June 1783, they built a huge hot-air balloon from paper and cloth. It was 30m in diameter and had a platform at the bottom for two passengers. Beneath the platform, on the ground, lay a fire to heat up the air that would carry the balloon into the sky.

The huge unmanned balloon rose 300m into the air, and landed 2km (1.24 miles) away. The passengers for the next flight, three months later, were a duck, a rooster and a sheep: a human volunteer went up a month later. Science teacher Piâtre de Rozier became the first man to travel in a balloon, although it was connected to the ground with a rope. The first free-floating flight took place on November 21. De Rozier and a French soldier named Marquis d'Arlandes flew 9 km (5.5 miles) through the air, for nearly half an hour.

Bad invention

Hydrogen was far more efficient than hot air, but it had one great disadvantage – it was highly inflammable. In the 1920s and 1930s great hydrogen-filled airships were built to ferry passengers across the Atlantic Ocean. In 1937, the German-built *Hindenburg* was coming in to land at Lakehurst, New Jersey, USA, when it burst into flames. The huge airship was destroyed in 30 seconds, and 35 passengers and crew were killed.

Discovery of hydrogen

The Montgolfiers' rival, Jacques Charles, flew a hydrogen balloon in August of 1783. His was made of silk and filled with hydrogen, a lighter-than-air gas, which did not need to be heated. On its first unmanned flight his balloon drifted from Paris to Gonesse, 24 km (15 miles) away. When it landed it was hacked to pieces by frightened peasants. A couple of weeks after the Montgolfier's first manned flight, Charles took himself and another passenger on a 43 km (27 mile) journey.

Army commanders such as Napoleon, realized that balloons would be brilliant observation platforms during a battle. But the balloon could not be steered and was dependent on air currents to move it along. Today, balloons remain something of a curiosity, although one did travel all the way around the world in 1999.

1709	1783	1785	1937	1978	1999
FATHER BARTOLOMEU DE GUSMÃO DEMONSTRATES THE IDEA OF THE HOT AIR BALLOON TO THE PORTUGUESE COURT	THE MONTGOLFIER BROTHERS INVENT THE FIRST MANNED AIR BALLOON JACQUES CHARLES INVENTS HYDROGEN BALLOON	FIRST CROSSING OF ENGLISH CHANNEL BY A BALLOON	*HINDENBURG* BURST INTO FLAMES KILLING 35 PEOPLE	FIRST CROSSING OF ATLANTIC OCEAN BY HOT-AIR BALLOON	BALLOON FLIES ALL THE WAY AROUND THE WORLD

Steam locomotive, 1804

The first steam engine was invented in Egypt, around 2000 years ago, though it was not until the early 18th century that the idea was put to practical use. Building on the work of Denis Papin and Thomas Savery, in 1712 an English inventor named Thomas Newcomen made a machine called the Atmospheric Steam-Engine. Designed to pump water from coalmines, it used steam produced by boiling water to drive a **piston**, which could be rapidly and repeatedly raised and lowered.

In 1769 Scottish instrument-maker James Watt devised a way of transforming the piston's up-and-down motion to circular motion, so it could turn a wheel. Steam engines were immediately put to use driving factory machinery, helping to make Britain the 19th century's richest and most powerful nation.

Rails and steam engines

Rails carrying wheeled vehicles had been used by the Ancient Greeks to haul boats over the narrow **isthmus** of Corinth. They were also used in European mines from as early as the 15th century. When Newcomen was inventing his steam engine, rails carrying horse-drawn coal wagons were a common feature in British mines.

Trevithick's locomotive Catch me who can *in London in 1808. The locomotive was a sensation, but failed to attract financial backing to develop the idea.*

Cornishman Richard Trevithick was the first to put steam engine and rails together. In 1804 he built a locomotive which carried 10 tons of iron and 70 men along the rail track at Pen-y-Darren in South Wales. In 1808 he brought a locomotive called *Catch me who can* to London, to find money to develop the idea. Though a major sensation, Trevithick attracted no backers. He gave up on locomotives, emigrated to Peru to work on **steam-powered** mining pumps, but died in poverty in 1833.

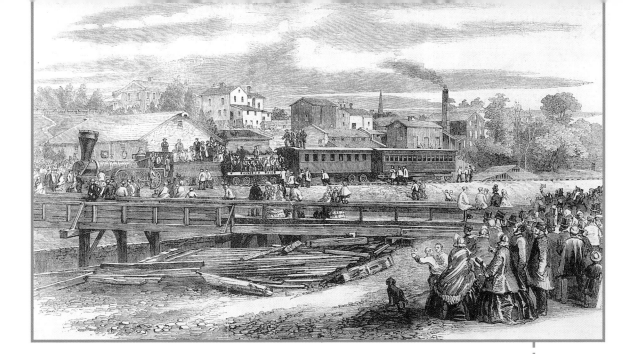

The coal industry

Trevithick's idea was developed in the coal mining industry. In 1825 engineer George Stephenson completed a 40km (25 mile) rail line between the coal-mining town of Darlington and the port of Stockton, in the northeast of England. A steam train of his own design hauled coal from pit to coast, where it could be taken around the country by boat. It also carried paying passengers.

In 1830 Stephenson completed the first inter-city line, between Liverpool and Manchester. The line had a two-way track, and ran to a daily timetable. The locomotives that pulled the carriages at 50kmph (30mph) were Stephenson's too. His design, the *Rocket,* had won a competition to find the best locomotive available.

Within 20 years, Britain was criss-crossed with railway lines. The idea caught on throughout the world. Rail provided cheap and fast travel over long distances for both goods and people. Today, steam trains have mostly been replaced by electric or diesel powered locomotives.

The arrival of the first train of the Atlantic and Great Western railroad at James Town from New York, 1860.

AD 00	1712	1804	1825	1994
FIRST STEAM ENGINE INVENTED	THOMAS NEWCOMEN'S ATMOSPHERIC STEAM-ENGINE PUMPS WATER FROM MINES	RICHARD TREVITHICK RUNS LOCOMOTIVE ON RAIL LINE AT PEN-Y-DARREN	GEORGE STEPHENSON BUILDS FIRST PUBLIC RAILWAY LINE FROM STOCKTON TO DARLINGTON	FIRST TRAINS TRAVEL BETWEEN UK AND FRANCE VIA CHANNEL TUNNEL

Bicycle, 1817

The first recognizable bicycle arrived in 1817. It was called a 'draisine', after its German inventor, Baron von Drais. His machine had two spoked-iron wheels connected by a cross bar, and a steering device. There were no pedals, but a rider could reach a speed of 15kmph (9.5 mph) by pushing along with the feet. A journey that would have taken a day's walk could now be done in two or three hours.

In many ways the draisine looked quite like a modern bicycle, though there was some way to go before the bike we know today was perfected. In 1842 Scottish blacksmith Kirkpatrick Macmillan made a bicycle with pedals, adapted from treadles (levers) which power sewing machines. Macmillan drove his bicycle 64km (40 miles) between Dumfries and Glasgow to prove its worth, but it never caught on. He lacked the ability to successfully publicize and exploit the idea.

Invented by Baron von Drais, the hobby-horse or draisine, could reach 15mph.

Setting the pace

Next came the 'vélocepède', a French word which means 'swift foot'. Invented by father and son Pierre and Ernest Michaux in 1861, it had pedals attached to a large front wheel. In the UK, it was called a 'boneshaker' because it was so uncomfortable to ride. Britain's James Starley developed Michaux's idea further in 1870. He attached his pedal directly to a much bigger front wheel, on a machine known as the 'Penny Farthing' (so called because the two British coins were relatively similar in proportion to the front and back wheel). This was difficult and dangerous to use, but reached an impressive speed of 30kmph (20mph).

And finally...

The final step in the development of the bicycle came in 1879 when Harry J Lawson fitted a chain to connect his pedals to the back wheel. This idea was taken up by a nephew of James Starley's named John K Starley. In 1885 he produced the 'Rover Safety bicycle'. It returned to von Drais's original idea of two wheels of the same size, which made it much safer to ride. This final design breakthrough produced a machine similar to a modern-day bicycle.

Modern-day bicycles are much lighter and stronger than earlier models, an example being this racing bike seen at the Sydney Olympics, 2000.

Further refinements, such as brakes, sprung saddles for extra comfort, lighter frames, and John Dunlop's much speedier **pneumatic tyres**, made bicycles an even greater success. They were cheap and pleasant to ride. They made travel so much easier they soon became enormously popular.

In the early 20th century, cars and motorbikes offered an even easier and speedier way of getting from A to B, and the popularity of the bicycle soon faded. But a combination of road **congestion**, pollution, and the keep-fit fashion of the late 20th century, has meant that the bike is almost as popular now as it was in its brief heyday, 100 years ago.

1817 THE DRAISINE – THE FIRST BICYCLE	**1842** KIRKPATRICK MACMILLAN'S BICYCLE WAS THE FIRST TO HAVE PEDALS	**1861** THE VÉLOCEPÈDE HAD PEDALS ATTACHED DIRECTLY TO THE FRONT WHEEL	**1870** JAMES STARLEY DEVELOPED THE PENNY FARTHING	**1885** JOHN K STARLEY'S 'ROVER SAFETY BICYCLE' HAD A CHAIN WHICH LINKED PEDALS TO WHEEL, AND WAS THE FIRST MODERN STYLE BICYCLE

Underground railway, 1863

The first underground railway in the world was built in London in 1863, as a response to traffic **congestion** and to provide transport into the city for **commuters** who lived outside the city. It was called the Metropolitan Railway and stretched from Paddington Station (the main railway line into London from the west), through several other mainline stations, to Farringdon.

The line was built with the 'cut and cover' technique of tunnel building. A broad trench was dug into the ground, the line was laid and a tunnel was built around it, and then covered over.

The Metropolitan Line used steam trains. Ventilation holes were regularly spaced along its length, and special **condensers** collected some of the smoke that billowed from the trains. It was a dirty, unpleasant experience.

Marc Isambard Brunel's tunnel shield. This machine made it possible to burrow under rivers, and paved the way for the deep tunnels that were built for the London underground.

Tunnels

Modern tunnelling began in 1818 when Marc Isambard Brunel invented a tunnelling device inspired by the shipworm insect *Terado navalis*, which burrowed into wood. Called the 'tunnel shield', it was a box-shaped iron case with cells for 33 miners to dig away in relative safety. A brick lining was built around the hole they made. Peter Barlow and James Henry Greathead developed this idea, and used cast-iron segments rather than bricks to build the lining of the tunnel. This method was used to make the deep tunnels of London's underground system.

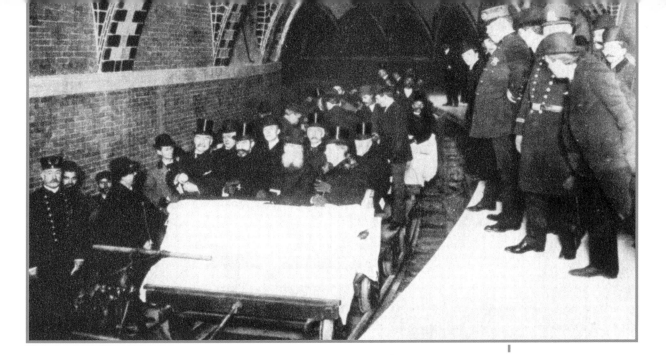

Electric trains

In 1879 Werner von Siemens unveiled an electric train at a Berlin Exhibition. Battery powered trains had been used before, with limited success, but Siemens' train took its power directly from a 'live' rail on the track. (This means the rail had electricity running though it.) It was fast, efficient, relatively quick and it was clean.

A deep, underground line was built for this new train between Stockwell in south London, and Bank, called 'The City and South London Railway'. Its fourteen electric locomotives each pulled three carriages, and could travel up and down the tracks at a rate of one train every four minutes. Each train could carry 100 passengers, and in its first year the line carried five million people.

Underground systems were then built in major cities all around the world. Paris opened its Metro in 1900, and New York began its Subway service in 1904. They are still the quickest way to get around a major city.

The opening of the New York subway in 1904 saw the Mayor of New York taking a tour of the first completed section.

1818	1863	1879	1887–1890	1900	1904
MARC ISAMBARD BRUNEL INVENTS TUNNEL SHIELD	THE WORLD'S FIRST UNDERGROUND SERVICE, THE METROPOLITAN LINE, OPENS IN LONDON	WERNER VON SIEMENS UNVEILS ELECTRIC POWERED TRAIN AT BERLIN EXHIBITION	CITY AND SOUTH LONDON LINE IS BUILT – THE FIRST UNDERGROUND LINE TO USE ELECTRIC TRAINS	PARIS METRO OPENS	NEW YORK SUBWAY OPENS

Motorbike, 1885

Invented at the same time as the car, the motorbike is essentially a bicycle with a motor attached to it. The first motorbike was **steam-powered**, and built in 1869. The weight of the **boiler** and steam engine, mounted on a French vélocepède bicycle (see page 24), must have made it very unstable. In 1884 L D Copeland of Philadelphia began manufacturing steam-powered tricycles. The third wheel made it less likely to topple over. Altogether, 200 were built.

Motorbikes and petrol

The first proper petrol-engine motorbike was made by the car inventor Gottlieb Daimler in 1885. It was a heavy, clumsy-looking vehicle, with the engine mounted high on the bike. In 1894 the German company Hildebrand and Wolfmüller began to make the 'Motorrad' – the first factory-produced bike.

By the early 1900s the design had settled into one we would recognize today. The wheels were the same size, the engine was mounted low on the body to make the bike more stable, and drove the back wheel with a chain or belt. 1903 saw the introduction of the sidecar and in 1904, **twist-grip throttles** were invented, which allowed the rider to control the speed of the bike by hand rather than foot. By 1914, the bike could go as fast as 150kmph (95mph). When the First World War began, speedy motorcyclists were soon used to carry messages to and from army headquarters.

One of the first factory-produced motorbikes. Their cost and ease of use made the first motorbikes at least as popular as the car.

A versatile machine

Motorbikes were cheaper to buy than cars, cheaper to run and easier to look after. They were also easier to manoeuvre and faster, but they were much more dangerous. Their small size made them difficult for a motorist to see, and gave the rider no protection from other vehicles or the weather. But in Britain, motorbikes were more popular than motorcars until the 1950s.

After the Second World War there was a '**baby boom**' in Europe and North America. The car was better for families, and the motorbike became less popular. The scooter became very popular during the 1950s, as did the moped, which returned to the motorbike's origins as a bicycle with a motor. The moped was originally developed in the Second World War for use by soldiers in hit and run raids. (Its lightness made it possible for men to carry it on their back.)

In more recent times, increased traffic **congestion** has made the motorbike more popular as it can weave in and out of city traffic jams. Police forces and courier companies still make widespread use of motorbikes for these reasons.

Popular with both the police and motorcycle gangs, the Harley Davidson is one of the most admired motorbikes of the 20th century. The first models were built in 1903.

1869	1884	1885	1894	1903
FIRST STEAM-POWERED MOTORBIKE	STEAM-POWERED TRICYCLE INVENTED	GOTTLIEB DAIMLER PRODUCED FIRST PETROL-ENGINE MOTORBIKE	HILDEBRAND AND WOLFMÜLLER MANUFACTURE THE 'MOTORRAD', THE FIRST FACTORY-PRODUCED BIKE	SIDECAR INVENTED

Motor car, 1886

Inventors had been trying to come up with a 'horseless carriage' for centuries. A primitive **steam-powered** cart may have trundled around China in 1662. French inventor Nicholas-Joseph Cugnot designed a lumbering, steam-powered carriage in 1770. It had a huge **boiler** at the front, and looked like a giant ant.

Fuel and the internal combustion engine

In the early 19th century new fuels such as coal gas became available. The **internal combustion engine** was developed to make use of this gas. But the real breakthrough came when German Karl Benz produced an internal combustion engine that used petrol, which at the time was an unwanted by-product of the oil **refinery** industry.

Internal combustion engine

An internal combustion engine works by exploding fuel to move a **piston**. The moving piston rotates a **crankshaft**, which can be made to turn the car wheels. The first was built by a Frenchman named Étienne Lenoir. He used a converted steam engine which exploded a mixture of air and coal gas to drive a piston. In 1876 Nikolaus Otto and Eugen Langen invented a gas-powered engine. In 1885 Karl Benz produced an engine which used petrol instead of gas. He also discovered that an electric spark was the best way to ignite his fuel. His engine was much lighter than gas-powered ones, which made it more suitable for a road vehicle.

In July 1886 Karl Benz fitted a petrol-driven engine to a three-wheeled carriage and drove it around his home town of Mannheim. A month later, two other German inventors, Gottlieb Daimler and Wilhelm Maybech, unveiled their four-wheel motor car which used the same type of engine. The first cars could travel little faster than a horse. By the turn of the century they could go as fast as 160kmph (100mph).

The internal combustion engine was soon put to use with many forms of transport such as the motorbike, bus and lorry, and farming machinery such as the tractor and **threshing machine**. It also led to the invention of the aeroplane and helicopter.

Improvements

Henry Ford decided to make cars in their millions, which gave ordinary people the freedom to go anywhere, at any time. Today, there are around 500 million cars in daily use around the world.

Since their arrival on the roads there have been many improvements. In 1892 the diesel engine was invented, then front-wheel steering instead of back-wheel steering was used, brakes were fitted to all four wheels, and gears and wheel **suspension** improved. Since the 1970s much greater attention has been paid to cutting down the pollution car engines cause, by making engines produce cleaner exhaust (gases expelled by an engine). But the basic design of a motor car is still fundamentally the same as it was 100 years ago.

Ford's Model T *production line in Detroit, 1913. The* Model T *was the first cheap, mass-produced car, and 15 million were built.*

1859	**1885**	**1886**	**1892**	**1909**
ÉTIENNE LENOIR INVENTS INTERNAL COMBUSTION ENGINE	KARL BENZ PRODUCES FIRST PETROL-DRIVEN INTERNAL COMBUSTION ENGINE	KARL BENZ INVENTS FIRST PETROL-DRIVEN CAR DAIMLER AND MAYBECH PRODUCE FIRST FOUR-WHEELED PETROL-DRIVEN CAR	DIESEL ENGINES INTRODUCED FOR CARS	HENRY FORD INVENTS THE 'PRODUCTION LINE' TO MASS-PRODUCE CARS

Aeroplane, 1903

On December 17 1903, two brothers named Wilbur and Orville Wright took their petrol-engine plane *Flyer I* into the air in Kitty Hawk, North Carolina. This first manned, powered flight was one of the great events of the 20th century. Although the flights on that day lasted no more than 60 seconds, the possibilities the *Flyer* offered were phenomenal.

Wilbur Wright (1867–1912) and Orville Wright (1871–1948)

Sons of a bishop, the Wright Brothers were brought up in Dayton, Ohio. They began their careers editing and printing a local newspaper, the Dayton *West Side News*. They also opened a business, repairing, selling and manufacturing bicycles. Both enterprises would finance their flying machine project. Wilbur died of typhoid fever in 1912, but Orville lived a long, prosperous life. The *Flyer* project cost the Wrights a mere $1000. (This is around £14,000 today.) Orville made over $500,000 from his invention, so it was an extremely successful investment.

The Wrights jealously guarded their claim to be the first people to fly. When American's foremost science museum, the Smithsonian, suggested they might not have made the first powered flight, Wilbur sent *Flyer I* to the Science Museum in London. The Smithsonian were only allowed to have it back if they promised never to contest the Wright's claim to be the first people to fly.

The first real breakthrough in aircraft design came in the early 19th century. A wealthy British inventor named Sir George Cayley spent much of his life making **gliders**. He built his first successful one in 1804, and by 1853 had made one big enough to carry a man 200m (600ft) in the air.

In 1848 another British inventor named John Stringfellow made a very short and shaky flight in a **steam-powered** flying machine. So did French engineer Clement Ader and American Hiram Maxim in the 1890s. American Professor Samuel P Langley in 1896 built an unmanned steam-powered model plane that was a sensation. The American Government gave him the then considerable sum of $50,000 to develop it further for the army, but his full-sized flying machines were unable to fly.

The Wright brothers

The Wright brothers were inspired to conquer the air by the death of Otto Lilienthal in a flying accident in 1896. Otto was one of two brothers who were making pioneering flights with gliders in Germany. The Wrights read up on the work of Cayley and the Lilienthals and set about improving existing designs.

Co-operating with their friend, engineer Octave Chanute, they built a series of gliders to test which aircraft shapes and control **mechanisms** worked best. They designed their own **propellers** and were able to power them with the recently developed petrol engine. Because it was lighter or more powerful than previously available power sources, it was capable of lifting itself, the plane, and a passenger into the air.

By 1905 they had built *Flyer III*, which could stay in the air for 40 minutes. It could also fly relatively complex manoeuvres, such as a figure of eight. They took out **patents** for their machine and sold it to the United States Army, and French manufacturers. The aeroplane became one of the most influential inventions of the century. It revolutionized travel, cutting journey times between countries from days or weeks to mere hours. In warfare, troops could now be attacked from the sky as well as the ground, and bombers had the power to bring destruction to cities hundreds of miles away from the fighting.

As Wilbur Wright runs behind him, Orville Wright makes the first successful powered flight. Flyer I was made of wood covered with cotton cloth. The twelve-horse-power engine turned two large wooden propellers.

1804	1848	1853	1891–1896	1903
SIR GEORGE CAYLEY MAKES FIRST SUCCESSFUL GLIDER	JOHN STRINGFELLOW MADE A FLIGHT IN A STEAM-POWERED PLANE	CAYLEY'S GLIDER MAKES A SUCCESSFUL FLIGHT WITH A MAN ON BOARD	AVIATION INVENTORS OTTO AND GUSTAV LILIENTHAL MAKE HUNDREDS OF PIONEERING GLIDER FLIGHTS UNTIL OTTO IS KILLED IN A FLYING ACCIDENT	FIRST FLIGHT BY THE WRIGHT BROTHERS

Jet, 1930

A hundred years ago the fastest way to get from New York to London was by steam liner. The trip took over a week. Today, the journey can be made by **supersonic** jet airliner in an extraordinary three hours.

The jet engine

The first aeroplanes used a **propeller** to pull them through the air. Some aircraft still use propellers today. But to go faster and higher, plane builders use a jet engine.

Frank Whittle, an apprentice in Britain's Royal Air Force (RAF), designed a working jet engine in the 1920s, which he called a 'turbojet'. The RAF wasn't interested in his jet, so he **patented** the idea himself in 1930. But by 1935, the British government feared they would soon be at war with Nazi Germany, and work on Whittle's jet engine went ahead. New metal alloys had been developed that could withstand the high temperatures generated by a continually running jet engine. Whittle had developed a full-size working engine by 1937. In 1941 a jet aircraft using this engine, called the *Gloster Meteor*, took to the skies.

How a jet works

This is a turbojet. It is used by all the fastest aircraft. The idea behind the jet engine is very simple.

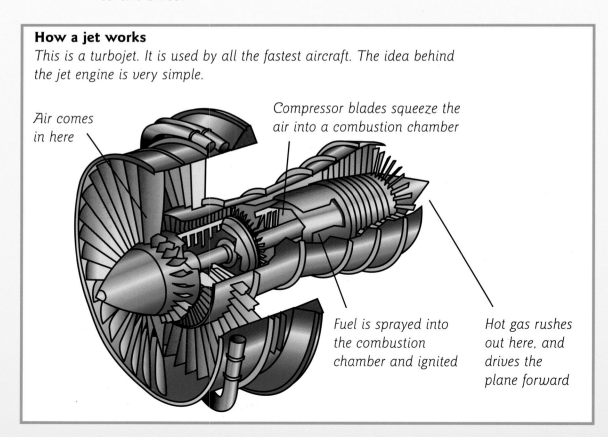

Air comes in here

Compressor blades squeeze the air into a combustion chamber

Fuel is sprayed into the combustion chamber and ignited

Hot gas rushes out here, and drives the plane forward

Not knowing of Whittle's work, German engineer Hans Joachim Pabst von Ohain had patented his own jet engine in 1935. The Nazi government was eager for von Ohain to develop his idea as it would be a very effective weapon. It was a great success. Although Whittle invented the first jet engine, the first jet plane to actually fly was the *Heinkel He 178*, which took to the sky in August 1939.

The Germans introduced several jet **combat aircraft** during the Second World War. The deadliest was the *Messerschmitt Me 262* – a twin-engine fighter plane that proved to be devastatingly effective against British and American warplanes.

When the war ended in 1945 another war seemed possible between Russia and America. This spurred more research into jet aircraft. In 1947 American jet pilot Chuck Yeager flew a rocket-propelled craft called the *Bell X-1* faster than the speed of sound (1220kmph (760 mph)). By the early 1960s jet fighters such as the British *Lightning*, the American *Phantom* and Russian *Mig-21* could all fly at twice this speed – covering a mile in less than three seconds.

Some modern military jets such as this F-3 Tornado can change the position of their wings. Here the wings are swept back – the best position for high-speed flight.

1930	1935	1939	1941	1947
FRANK WHITTLE PATENTS THE TURBOJET ENGINE	HANS JOACHIM PABST VON OHAIN PATENTS HIS OWN JET ENGINE DESIGN	THE *HEINKEL HE 178*, THE WORLD'S FIRST JET AIRCRAFT, TAKES TO THE SKY	FIRST FLIGHT OF BRITISH JET AIRCRAFT – GLOSTER METEOR	CHUCK YEAGER FLIES THE *BELL X-1* FASTER THAN THE SPEED OF SOUND

Helicopter, 1936

The idea of a wingless vehicle, thrust through the air by a revolving rotor, has been around for at least 1600 years. The Ancient Chinese had a spinning toy which flew straight into the air, called a 'flying top'. Italian artist Leonardo da Vinci sketched out an idea for a 'flying screw' in 1480, which resembled the idea of helicopter design but he mistakenly imagined a man would be able to turn the rotor fast enough to lift it into the air.

Focke's FA-61. In 1938, legendary German test pilot Hanna Reitsch made a vertical landing of Focke's machine inside the Berlin Olympic Stadium, demonstrating the helicopter's great advantage over the aeroplane.

Early 20th-century attempts

The arrival of the **internal combustion engine** enabled the helicopter's development. In 1907 Frenchman Paul Cornu managed to get his **prototype** helicopter to take off. It wobbled two metres (6ft) in the air for a hair-raising twenty seconds. When the engine cut out, it crashed to the ground and collapsed.

In 1923 Spanish inventor Juan de la Cierva flew a strange helicopter-plane, which he called an 'autogiro'. This had a **propeller** at the front (like most aircraft of that era), but instead of wings it had long flapping rotors. As the propeller pulled it along, the rotors spun, and lifted it into the air. These rotors were hinged, and could move up and down, allowing the pilot to control the direction of flight.

D-EBVU

The first real helicopters

The Germans developed the first real helicopter. Professor Heinriche Focke designed the *Focke-Achgelis FA-61*, which first flew in 1936. It had the shape of a plane, but instead of wings there were two rotors held above the body of the plane. It could take off and land vertically, and hover in the air.

In America, Russian immigrant and helicopter designer Igor Sikorsky was watching these developments closely. In 1939 he took his own helicopter, the *VS-300*, into the air. It had all the features of most helicopters today. A single main rotor was placed behind the pilot, and another smaller one on the tail.

Helicopters were first used as **military** aircraft by the US Navy in 1943. They were perfect for rescue missions, plucking men from the sea, or delivering and collecting men and supplies in hard-to-reach places. Since the 1960s helicopters fitted with missiles and machine guns have been used to attack infantry and tanks.

AD 400	1480	1907	1923	1936	1939
CHINESE INVENT 'FLYING TOP' TOY	LEONARDO DA VINCI SKETCHES 'FLYING SCREW'	PAUL CORNU FLIES PROTOTYPE HELICOPTER FOR 20 SECONDS	JUAN DE LA CIERVA FLIES AUTOGIRO	PROFESSOR HEINRICHE FOCKE'S TWIN ROTOR *FOCKE-ACHGELIS FA-61* MAKES FIRST FLIGHT	IGOR SIKORSKY MAKES FIRST FLIGHT IN *VS-300*, THE FIRST MODERN HELICOPTER

Hovercraft, 1955

The concept of a hovercraft – a vehicle that floats on a cushion of air – has been around since the 17th century. British inventor John Thornycroft worked on the idea in the 1870s, but did not have an engine light and strong enough to power his design. The hovercraft had to wait for the invention of the **internal combustion engine** before it could be properly developed.

Christopher Cockerell

English inventor Christopher Cockerell was the first to build a working hovercraft. His initial design involved a combination of empty tins of cat food and coffee, and a vacuum cleaner motor which had been altered to blow rather than suck. Cockerell's model clearly showed that a vessel could be lifted up by a cushion of air, and he **patented** it in 1955.

Next, he built a radio-controlled model. Government officials in 1956 thought it was such a sensation they ordered it to be kept secret, and developed as a weapon. But the Navy thought it was a plane, and the airforce thought it was a boat. Both felt the other should take responsibility for it. The army wasn't interested at all. After three years Cockerell was allowed to take his invention to **private industry** to see what they could do with it.

Cockerell's SR.N1, the world's first working hovercraft. The machine's ability to travel at speed over water and move from land to water with ease, caused a sensation.

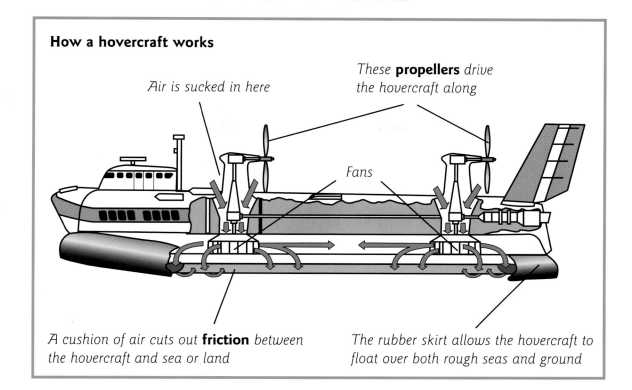

How a hovercraft works

Air is sucked in here

*These **propellers** drive the hovercraft along*

Fans

*A cushion of air cuts out **friction** between the hovercraft and sea or land*

The rubber skirt allows the hovercraft to float over both rough seas and ground

SR.N1

The first working hovercraft was built in 1959 by helicopter manufacturers Saunders Roe. They called it SR.N1 and Cockerell demonstrated its unique ability to travel smoothly between land and sea by driving it off the beach at Dover and across the Channel to Calais.

The SR.N1 only worked when the ground or sea it travelled over was very flat. This problem was solved when inventor C H Latimer-Needham devised a rubberized 'skirt' which raised the hovercraft higher off the ground. This enabled the hovercraft to plough through choppy sea and rough ground much more effectively.

Although hovercraft are now found all over the world, they never became as widely used as people imagined. Trains, boats, cars and planes still do their job at least as well as a hovercraft.

1955	1959	1961	1968
AFTER BUILDING A WORKING MODEL THE PREVIOUS YEAR, CHRISTOPHER COCKERELL PATENTS HIS HOVERCRAFT DESIGN	FIRST FULL SIZE HOVERCRAFT BUILT. COCKERELL PILOTS IT ACROSS THE CHANNEL	C H LATIMER-NEEDHAM INVENTS RUBBER SKIRT WHICH ALLOWS HOVERCRAFT TO TRAVEL ON SEA IN ROUGH WEATHER	HOVERCRAFT PASSENGER AND CAR SERVICE ACROSS ENGLISH CHANNEL BEGINS

Supertanker, 1956

Supertankers, officially known as 'Ultra Large Crude Carriers', are among the biggest mobile objects ever built. The *Seawise Giant*, for example, would be taller than the twin towers of the World Trade Centre in New York if it could be placed upright on its **stern**.

The first oil tanker

The first oil tanker was built in 1886, a year after the invention of the petrol-powered **internal combustion engine**. Petrol comes from crude oil (oil in its natural state in the ground) and much of this is found in inaccessible parts of the world such as the Middle East, Alaska and Siberia. By the 1930s, petrol was in great demand. Although pipelines can be built to move oil from where it is found to where it is needed, the most economic way of transporting it is by sea.

An international crisis led to the creation of the first supertankers. Egypt has a waterway called the Suez Canal, which links the Mediterranean Sea with the Red Sea. Without this canal, tankers travelling from the oil-rich Middle Eastern nations would have to go all the way around Africa to get to Europe. In 1956 and between 1967 and 1975 the canal was closed because of wars between Egypt and other nations.

Many supertankers are too big for ports. This one is unloading its cargo of crude oil at a 'single point mooring' (SPM). Oil unloaded here is carried by pipeline to a refinery.

Practicalities

Around this time new ship building techniques were being developed. Oil companies were able to have huge oil tankers built to carry more oil per journey and cut the cost of transporting it, especially if they had to go all the way around Africa. Large, pre-fabricated sections could be welded together making construction much easier and quicker.

Tankers are very simple vessels. The engine and crew quarters are in the stern, where any fire would be less likely to spread to the highly inflammable oil. The **cargo**-holds, where the oil is kept, are separated by many bulkheads (partitions) to stop the liquid cargo from forming waves inside the **hull**. Such wave motion with thousands of tons of oil could cause serious damage to the tanker.

The deck of a supertanker. Although these vessels are vast, they are very simple ships to sail and operate, and only need a small crew.

Risk of pollution

The history of supertankers is littered with accidents. In 1989, for example, the supertanker *Exxon Valdez* ran aground in Alaska. It leaked oil for two days, polluting 1770 km (1100 miles) of coastline and killing many thousands of sea birds. There is a great deal of public concern about the safety of supertankers. Today, a typical supertanker carries around nearly 40 million gallons of oil (around 2000 tons). On board, computers monitor the location and direction of the ship, and collision-avoidance **radar** continually monitor the possibility of a crash with other ships.

1885	1886	1956 ONWARDS	1978	1989
INVENTION OF THE PETROL-POWERED INTERNAL COMBUSTION ENGINE PUTS PETROL IN DEMAND	FIRST OIL TANKER BUILT	FIRST SUPERTANKERS BUILT FOLLOWING CLOSURE OF SUEZ CANAL	*AMOCO CADIZ* SINKS OFF FRENCH COAST, CAUSING TERRIBLE POLLUTION	OIL SPILL FROM THE *EXXON VALDEZ* POLLUTES HUGE PART OF ALASKAN COASTLINE

Jumbo jet, 1969

Jet aircraft were developed during the Second World War, and were very expensive to build and fly. The British *De Havilland Comet* was the first jet airliner, but in its first year of carrying passengers in 1952, two of the jets fell out of the sky, and it was grounded for several years.

American manufacturers Boeing built a bigger and faster airliner called the 707. It was a four-engine jet that could take up to 180 passengers across the Atlantic at 900kmph (600mph). Boeing realized that they should design bigger planes to carry hundreds of passengers – more passengers mean more money for fuel.

The bigger the better

In 1966 Boeing unveiled plans for the Boeing 747, swiftly named the 'Jumbo' because of its huge size. It made its first flight in 1969, and began to carry fare-paying passengers in 1970. It could carry between 385 and 500 passengers up to 13,000km (8000 miles).

The Jumbo has four 'turbofan' engines, which combine powerful **propulsion** with low fuel consumption. They are also relatively quiet and cause less pollution than conventional 'turbojet' engines. The low fuel consumption also means that the Jumbo is ideal for long-distance journeys. It can fly between London and Tokyo, for example, without the need for a refuelling stop.

Jumbo jets have been so successful airports have had to lengthen their runways and redesign their passenger facilities to accommodate these huge aircraft.

A Boeing 747 carrying a NASA space shuttle. The shuttle made its first flight when it was launched from the back of a Jumbo jet.

Today's Jumbo

Today, the engines of the Jumbo burn even less fuel, and cause less air and noise pollution, and are now controlled by digital electronics and computer displays. The first 747s had a mind-boggling 971 dials and lights and gauges on the flight deck. Now there are only 365.

Jumbos also make up a third of the world's **cargo**-carrying aircraft. They also ferry troops to trouble spots around the world, and carry Space shuttles for NASA. In 1990, two 747s became the official overseas transport for the president of the United States.

Jumbo facts

- Each Jumbo jet is made of more than six million parts.
- The Jumbo has made Boeing more than $100 billion.
- In 30 years of flying the world's air routes, the 747 has carried enough passengers to make up a quarter of the world's population.
- Each Jumbo has 18 tyres — 16 on the central fuselage, and two on the nose wheel.
- The tail of a Jumbo is 19.41m (63ft 8") — the same size as a six-storey building.

1952	1963	1969	1977	1990
DE HAVILLAND COMET BECOMES FIRST JET AIRLINER TO CARRY PASSENGERS	BOEING BEGINS TO DEVELOP IDEA OF LARGE, WIDE-BODIED JET	FIRST FLIGHT OF BOEING 747	JUMBO JET USED TO TEST SPACE SHUTTLE	PRESIDENT OF THE UNITED STATES BEGINS TO USE 747 AS HIS OFFICIAL OVERSEAS TRANSPORT

Timeline

50,000BC	Evidence of the first boats – dugout canoes, powered by paddles
10,000BC	First log bridges in use
5000BC	Paved streets in the city of Ur
3500BC	Wheel invented in Mesopotamia and Sumeria
2000BC	Horses harnessed to wheeled vehicles
1500BC	Oar invented. It is three times more efficient than the paddle.
c. 500BC–AD 476	Roman civilization builds the finest roads in the ancient world
c. 400BC	Pillar and beam bridges in use in middle East
c. 300BC	Romans invent pozzolana, a water-proof cement
AD 00	First steam engine invented
1620	Cornelius van Drebel's oar-powered submarine makes its first voyage
1709	Father Bartolomeu de Gusmão demonstrates the idea of the hot air balloon to the Portuguese court
1783	The Montgolfier brothers invent the first manned air balloon Jacques Charles invents hydrogen balloon
1804	Richard Trevithick runs locomotive on rail line at Pen-y-Darren Sir George Cayley makes first successful **glider**
1807	Robert Fulton introduces first steamship passenger service between New York and Albany
1816	John Loudon McAdam develops three-layer road, which is adopted throughout Europe
1817	The draisine – the first bicycle
1825	George Stephenson builds first public railway line from Stockton to Darlington
1841	Invention of woven iron cable makes possible development of modern suspension bridges
1859	Étienne Lenoir invents **internal combustion engine**
1863	The Metropolitan Line, the world's first underground service, opens in London

1869	First **steam-powered** motorbike
1879	Werner von Siemens unveils electric powered train at Berlin Exhibition
1884	Charles Parsons invents the **steam turbine**
1885	Gottlieb Daimler produced first petrol-engine motorbike
	Karl Benz produces first petrol-driven internal combustion engine
	Invention of the petrol-powered internal combustion engine puts petrol in demand
1886	Karl Benz invents first petrol-driven car
	Gottlieb Daimler and Wilhelm Maybech produce first four-wheeled petrol-driven car
	First oil tanker built
1887–1890	City and South London line is built – the first underground line to use electric trains
1888	John Dunlop invents the **pneumatic tyre**
1903	First flight by the Wright Brothers
1909	Henry Ford invents the 'production line' to mass-produce cars
1930	Frank Whittle patents the turbojet engine
1939	The *Heinkel He 178*, the world's first jet aircraft, takes to the sky
	Igor Sikorsky makes first flight in *VS-300*, the first modern helicopter
1955	After building a working model the previous year, Christopher Cockerell patents his hovercraft design
1956	First supertankers built following closure of Suez Canal
1959	First full size hovercraft built. Cockerell pilots it across the channel.
1969	First flight of Boeing 747
1999	Balloon flies all the way around the world

Glossary

axle a pole on which a wheel revolves

baby boom period in history when the number of babies being born is very high

boiler container for boiling liquid, usually water

cargo goods carried by a ship, or other form of transport

cavalry soldiers on horseback

coffer dam water-proof box built on a river-bottom, to allow for building of foundations for a bridge

combat aircraft aircraft carrying weapons

commuters people who travel into a city to work

condenser device which filters and compresses a substance such as steam

congestion over-crowding, especially said of roads with too many cars on them

crankshaft a revolving shaft in an engine, driven by pistons

domesticate make tame enough for humans to keep without danger to themselves

empire a collection of territories controlled by another country

friction a force in contact with a moving object, which slows it down

glider a flying machine that does not use an engine

hull the main body of a boat

Industrial Revolution period of history, especially in Britain, when many people moved from the countryside and farms to work in factories and live in cities

internal combustion engine a device which uses a fuel such as burning gas or petrol mixed with air, to turn a crankshaft, which can then be used to power a machine or vehicle

irrigate supply land with water through artificial channels in fields

isthmus narrow strip of land surrounded by the sea, linking two larger bits of land

keel essential part of frame of boat, onto which other parts of the hull are attached

mechanism usually the moving parts in a machine

military to do with the armed forces – the army, navy or airforce

network a number of things which are linked, such as roads and railways

nuclear power power which makes use of the energy inside atoms

patent an official document confirming ownership of a particular invention

periscope a device containing mirrors inside a hollow tube, which enables the user to see what is above them – especially useful in submerged submarines to see above the surface

pioneer someone who is first, or among the first, to do a particular activity

piston a cylinder in an engine which moves up and down to power the crankshaft

pivot a small shaft or pin that supports something that turns, such as an oar on the side of a boat

pneumatic tyres rubber tyres filled with high-pressure air, to provide a smoother, more comfortable ride for a motor car, or other forms of transport

private industry businesses which make things for profit

propeller a device used by boats or aircraft, with blades connected to a central hub. When turned in water or air, a propeller drives a vehicle along.

propulsion the business of moving something along, especially a vehicle

prototype the first version of a device such as a vehicle or machine

radar high-frequency radio waves used to detect the position of distant objects, such as ships and aircraft

refinery a factory where a raw material, such as crude oil, is changed into other useful materials, such as petrol

steam-power an engine which uses steam to move a vehicle or power a machine

steam turbine a form of steam engine which uses high-pressure steam to turn a turbine – a wheel-like device made up of many blades

stern the back of a boat

supersonic flying faster than sound

suspension the mechanism which connects the wheels of a vehicle to the rest of it

threshing machine a farm machine used to thresh crops (that is, remove grain from the husks and straw)

torpedoes self-propelled tube-like weapons, containing explosives, launched from submarines

turnpike a barrier set across a road, which can be passed once a fee has been paid

twist-grip throttle a hand-operated device on a motorbike, which enables the rider to accelerate by turning it

Index

Titles in the *GREAT INVENTIONS* series include:

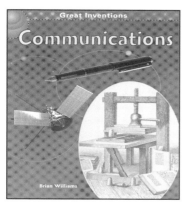

Hardback   0 431 13240 2

Hardback   0 431 13241 0

Hardback   0 431 13233 X

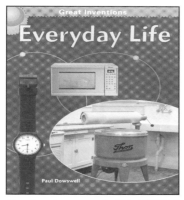

Hardback   0 431 13232 1

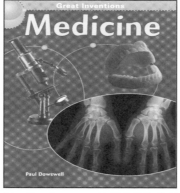

Hardback   0 431 13230 5

Hardback   0 431 13242 9

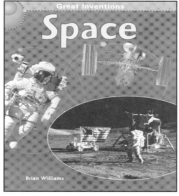

Hardback   0 431 13243 7

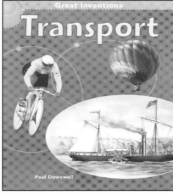

Hardback   0 431 13231 3

Find out about the other titles in this series on our website www.heinemann.co.uk/library